D0466270

DIEGO RODRIQUEZ DE SILVA Y **VELASQUEZ**
WAS BORN IN SEVILLE, SPAIN, ON JUNE 6, 1599, ONE
HUNDRED AND SEVEN YEARS AFTER CHRISTOPHER COLUMBUS
LEFT THAT CITY TO SAIL TO THE AMERICAS.

AS A SMALL CHILD, DIEGO'S DRAWINGS WERE SO GOOD
THAT HIS PARENTS SENT HIM TO STUDY WITH MASTER
PAINTER FRANCISCO HERRERA. BUT DIEGO SOON WANTED
A GREATER FREEDOM SO HE JOINED THE STUDIO OF
FRANCISCO PACHECO, A TEACHER WHO ALLOWED HIM
CREATIVE ARTISTIC FREEDOM. FROM THIS GREAT TEACHER
HE LEARNED THE FINE ART OF PAINTING AS WELL AS
LITERATURE AND PHILOSOPHY. FIVE YEARS LATER, AT
THE AGE OF 20, DIEGO MARRIED
JUANA, HIS TEACHER'S DAUGHTER.

AFTER RENDERING THREE
PORTRAITS OF KING PHILIP IV
YOUNG VELASQUEZ, AT THE
AGE OF 25, WAS APPOINTED THE
KING'S PAINTER. WITH HIS WIFE
AND TWO DAUGHTERS, HE LIVED
A HAPPY LIFE AT COURT WITH
PLENTY OF TIME TO FULFILL
HIS OCCUPATION AS ARTIST TO
THE ROYAL HOUSEHOLD.

VELASQUEZ PAINTED 121
OUTSTANDING CANVASES
AND BECAME ADVISOR AND
FRIEND TO HIS KING. HE DIED
AT THE AGE OF 61, RECOGNIZED
AS A GREAT ARTIST.

PORTRAIT OF VELASQUEZ BY ERNEST RABOFF

DIEGO RODRIGUEZ DE SILVA Y VELASQUEZ COMBINED THE ARTS OF DIPLOMACY AND PAINTING.

HE BELIEVED IN NATURE AND IN ART, AND THEY WERE HIS TWO COMPANIONS, HIS CLOSEST FRIENDS, IN HIS CREATIVE AND PEACEFUL LIFE.

VELASQUEZ SAID: " I WOULD RATHER BE AN ORDINARY PAINTER WORKING FROM LIFE THAN BE THE GREATEST COPYIST ON EARTH."

WHEN HE WAS ACCUSED OF PAINTING ONLY HEADS (PORTRAITS) HE SAID:"THAT IS VERY HIGH PRAISE. I KNOW HARDLY ANYONE WHO KNOWS HOW TO PAINT A HEAD."

HIS PAINTINGS SHOWED BOTH THE REALITY AND THE DREAMS OF HIS TIMES. THIS DEDICATION TO TRUTH IN ART BROUGHT HIM FAME IN HIS LIFETIME.

FROM HIS DEVOTION TO ART CAME THE COM-PASSION AND UNDERSTAND-ING THAT MADE HIM POPULAR WITH BOTH KINGS AND COMMONERS.

PORTRAIT OF VELASQUEZ (DETAIL FROM "THE MAIDS OF HONOR")

DEDICATED TO SID DORFMAN WHOSE ENCOURAGEMENT I
APPRECIATE AND WHOSE FRIENDSHIP I VALUE.

WORLD RIGHTS RESERVED BY ERNEST RABOFF AND GEMINI SMITH, INC.

LIBRARY OF CONGRESS CATALOGUE CARD NO. 74-121783   PRINTED IN JAPAN BY TOPPAN

DIEGO RODRIGUEZ DE SILVA Y VELASQUEZ

By Ernest Raboff

ART FOR CHILDREN

A GEMINI SMITH BOOK

EDITED BY BRADLEY SMITH

PUBLISHED BY
DOUBLEDAY & CO., INC.

GARDEN CITY, NEW YORK

PRINCE BALTASAR CARLOS, THE PRADO, MADRID

COVER:

PRINCE BALTASAR CARLOS,

SON OF KING PHILIP IV OF SPAIN,

WAS SIX YEARS OLD WHEN VELASQUEZ PAINTED

HIM RIDING HIS PRANCING PONY.

DETAIL FROM PAINTING

DON ANTONIO EL INGLES   PRADO, MADRID

THE "OLD WOMAN COOKING EGGS" BRINGS TOGETHER
REALISM AND BEAUTY. THE PAINTING IS LIKE
A HANDFUL OF SPARKLING GEMS.

THE ARTIST HAS PAINTED HIS MODELS IN A BRIGHT LIGHT.
ONCE OUR EYES HAVE ADJUSTED TO IT WE CAN STUDY THE
DETAILS FORM BY FORM, LINE BY LINE, COLOR BY COLOR.

DETAIL FROM PAINTING

VELASQUEZ FIRST LEADS OUR
EYES AROUND THE PAINTING
WITH HIS BRILLIANT EFFECTS
LIKE SPINNING PINWHEELS.
THE SMALL PINWHEEL INCLUDES
EGGS, COOKING PAN, THE
BOWL WITH A KNIFE AND ITS
CRESCENT SHADOW, THE
MORTAR AND PESTLE, THE HAND
HOLDING THE EGG, AND THE
HAND POISED WITH THE
WOODEN SPOON.

TO OUR EYES, A LARGER WHEEL
ENCIRCLES THIS CENTER AND
MOVES FROM THE COOK TO THE
BOY, TO THE PUMPKIN, ONION, WATER
PITCHERS, HANGING KETTLES, AND TO
THE CLOTH-DRAPED BASKET AT THE TOP.

SO LET OUR EYES TRACE THESE INTERESTING
CIRCLES. THE MORE WE USE OUR EYES, THE
MORE WE WILL LEARN
OF PAINTING AND OF LIFE ITSELF.

OLD WOMAN COOKING EGGS   NATIONAL GALLERY OF SCOTLAND, EDINBURGH

"PHILIP IV ON HORSEBACK" SHOWS US THE VAST KNOWLEDGE VELASQUEZ HAD OF MEN AND OF HORSES. BOTH FIGURES ARE POWERFUL AND ALIVE WITH ACTION YET ARE MASTERFULLY BALANCED BY THE ARTIST SO ONE DOES NOT OVERSHADOW THE OTHER.

DETAIL:
PHILIP IV

STUDY THE TWO HEADS. STUDY THE POSTURE OF THE RIDER AND THE POSITION OF THE HORSE. NOTICE HOW VELASQUEZ COMPARES THE SPARKLING ARMOR OF THE KING TO THE GLISTENING BROWN COAT OF HIS MOUNT.

DETAIL

THIS GREAT PORTRAIT ARTIST URGES US TO USE OUR EYES TO LEARN OF MEN, HORSES, AND ALL OF LIFE

PHILIP IV ON HORSEBACK   PRADO, MADRID

"QUEEN ISABELLA ON HORSEBACK" WAS PAINTED TO MATCH THE PORTRAITS OF HER HUSBAND, KING PHILIP IV, AND HER SON, BALTASAR CARLOS, BOTH OF WHOM WERE SHOWN ON HORSEBACK. BY LOOKING CAREFULLY AT THE HORSE'S HEAD AND THE RAISED HOOF, YOU CAN SEE THE ARTIST'S FIRST PAINTED OUTLINES. HE OFTEN REPAINTED DETAILS IN HIS CONSTANT STRIVING FOR PERFECTION.

QUEEN ISABELLA WAS THE MOTHER OF PRINCESS MARIA TERESA WHO BECAME QUEEN OF FRANCE.

IN THIS GRACEFUL PICTURE, THE QUEEN'S RIDING SKIRT, HER ARMS, THE HORSE'S NECK AND PRANCING LEG, EVEN THE CLOUDS AND THE SLOPING HILLS CURVE SOFTLY.

VELASQUEZ WAS DEDICATED TO REALITY AND DISCIPLINED HIMSELF TO PAINTING PRECISELY WHAT HE SAW.

HE SAW THE WORLD AS IT WAS AND LOVED IT.

HIS JOY IN NATURE AND HUMAN BEINGS ILLUMINATES EVERY PAINTING AND BRIGHTENS THOSE MOMENTS EACH OF US SPENDS IN STUDYING THEM.

QUEEN ISABELLA ON HORSEBACK   PRADO, MADRID

IN "TWO MEN AT A TABLE", VELASQUEZ HAS COMBINED
TWO SEPARATE SCENES INTO ONE PICTURE BY
RELATING THE COLORS AND SHAPES.

DETAIL: ORANGE ON VASE

IN THE STILL LIFE ON THE LEFT, OUR GAZE MOVES FROM
THE BRIGHT ORANGE DOWN THE GOLDEN CURVE OF THE URN
UPON WHICH IT RESTS TO THE UPSIDE-DOWN BRASS MORTAR.
THE PESTLE IN THE FRONT OF THE PICTURE LEADS TO THE
BOWLS STACKED TO DRY UPON ITS BROAD END. THESE
DIRECT OUR EYES TO THE SMALLER GREEN JUG. THE
EDGES OF THE TABLE FRAME THIS GROUP WHILE SEPARATING
IT FROM THE SCENE WITH THE TWO MEN.

IN THIS SECOND SCENE, THE MAN ON THE RIGHT LEANS
FORWARD DIRECTING US TOWARD THE STILL LIFE. EVEN THE
COLOR OF HIS COAT BRINGS US BACK ACROSS THE WHITE
CLOTH TO THE TABLE ON THE LEFT.

NOTICE THE BALANCE, THE HARMONY OF FORM AND COLOR
BETWEEN THE VASE WITH THE ORANGE IN ITS MOUTH AND
THE MAN WITH THE BOWL RAISED TO HIS LIPS.

IN THIS BOLD COMPOSITION THERE ARE MANY
DIFFERENT PATHS FOR OUR EYES TO EXPLORE.

TWO MEN AT A TABLE

VICTORIA AND ALBERT MUSEUM, CROWN COPYRIGHT

"THE WATER SELLER" WAS PAINTED BY VELASQUEZ IN HIS EARLY TWENTIES.

NOTICE THE SIMPLE STRENGTH OF THE DIAGONAL BALANCE IN THIS MASTERFUL COMPOSITION

DETAIL: BOY'S HEAD

VELASQUEZ RELATES THE WATER SELLER'S CLOSE CROPPED HEAD AND HIS DEEPLY WRINKLED FACE TO THE SMALLER, DENTED CONTAINER OPPOSITE HIM.

THEN THE ARTIST COMPARES THE SMOOTH-SKINNED, FIRM FEATURES OF THE YOUTH WITH THE FULL, ROUNDED FORM OF THE LARGE URN IN FRONT.

IT IS A PERFECT BALANCE

THESE VISUAL LINES CROSS AND FOCUS OUR EYES ON THE WATER GLASS.

DETAIL: LARGE URN

THE YOUNG BOY AND THE CRAFTSMAN TOGETHER HOLD THE GLASS. IT SEEMS TO SHOW US THAT THE TIME WHICH SEPARATES THEIR YEARS IS AS SHORT AS THE CRYSTAL STEM THAT LINKS THEIR HANDS.

THE WATER SELLER   VICTORIA AND ALBERT MUSEUM , CROWN COPYRIGHT

"THREE MUSICIANS" IS ANOTHER OF THE PAINTINGS
THAT VELASQUEZ PAINTED BETWEEN THE AGES OF 18 AND 21.

THESE YOUTHFUL PAINTINGS TELL A STORY.

IN THIS ONE WE CAN LEARN ABOUT SOME OF THE INSTRUMENTS
PEOPLE PLAYED AT THE BEGINNING OF THE 17TH CENTURY.

WE CAN STUDY THE CLOTHING, THE HAIR STYLES, AND
THE SHAPES OF THE DRINKING GLASSES OF THE TIME
WHEN THE ARTIST LIVED.

VELASQUEZ WARMS THE HAPPY SCENE WITH
GLOWING YELLOW COLORS.

THE BOY, WITH HIS PET MONKEY LOOKING OVER HIS
SHOULDER, SEEMS ALMOST TO INVITE US TO JOIN
THE FUN AND TO SHARE THE FOOD AND DRINK.

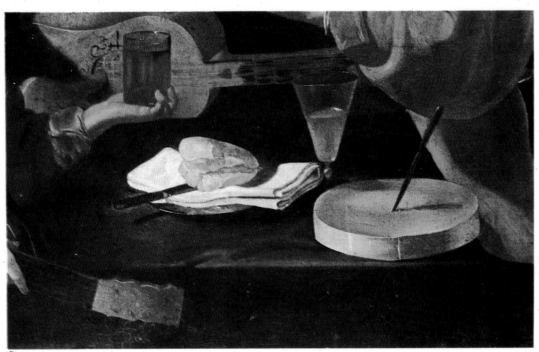

DETAIL: TABLE FROM "THREE MUSICIANS"

THREE MUSICIANS   STAATLICHE MUSEUM, BERLIN

"JUAN DE PAREJA" WAS VELASQUEZ'S SERVANT AND PUPIL. HE ASSISTED THE ARTIST BY GRINDING PAINTS, CLEANING BRUSHES, AND WHEN NECESSARY WAS A WELCOME TRAVELING COMPANION.

AT THE AGE OF 45, PAREJA GREATLY SURPRISED VELASQUEZ BY TURNING OUT HIS OWN FINE PAINTINGS.

BY CAREFULLY STUDYING PAREJA'S SHINING EYES IN THIS PAINTING, WE CAN GET AN IDEA OF THE BOND OF FRIENDSHIP AND RESPECT BETWEEN THESE TWO MEN.

THIS PORTRAIT INSPIRES US WITH ITS QUIET STRENGTH. THE BRONZED GLOW OF PAREJA'S OPEN, INTELLIGENT FACE IS HIGHLIGHTED BY THE SNOW-WHITE COLLAR AND THE SENSITIVELY PAINTED FOLDS OF THE RICH BROWN TUNIC AND CAPE.

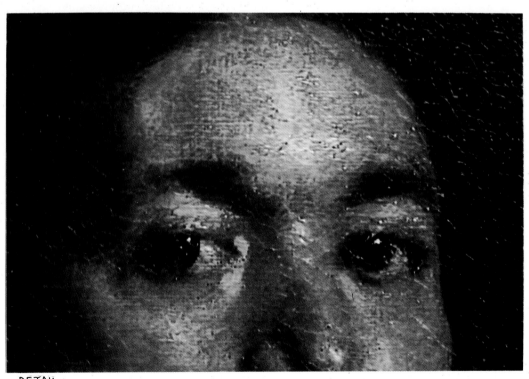

DETAIL

JUAN DE PAREJA   PRIVATE COLLECTION

"THE TAPESTRY WEAVERS" OR THE SPINNERS WERE TALENTED WOMEN WHO, WITH THEIR SPINNING WHEELS AND LOOMS, WOVE THE BEAUTIFUL **WALL HANGINGS** FOR THE ROYAL COURT.

VELASQUEZ PAINTED THEM WITH GENTLE REALISM, SHOWING THE GRACE OF THEIR ARMS AND LEGS, THE CURVES OF THEIR SHOULDERS, AND THE QUIET CONTENTMENT IN THEIR FACES.

STARTING WITH THE WOMAN IN THE LEFT FOREGROUND,

OUR GAZE SWEEPS ACROSS THE FRONT OF THE PAINTING. THEN VELASQUEZ DRAWS OUR ATTENTION FROM THE TWO WOMEN ON THE RIGHT INTO THE BACKGROUND SCENE THROUGH THE USE OF LIGHT.

THE SEPARATE SCENES OF ACTION MOVE AROUND THE WOMAN KNEELING IN THE CENTER.

DETAIL: WOMAN AT SPINNING WHEEL

THE TAPESTRY WEAVERS   PRADO, MADRID

"MARIANA OF AUSTRIA, QUEEN OF SPAIN" WAS PHILIP IV's
SECOND WIFE. SHE WAS MOTHER OF THE INFANTA MARGARITA,
PRINCE PHILIP PROSPER, AND CHARLES II, HEIR TO THE
THRONE OF SPAIN.

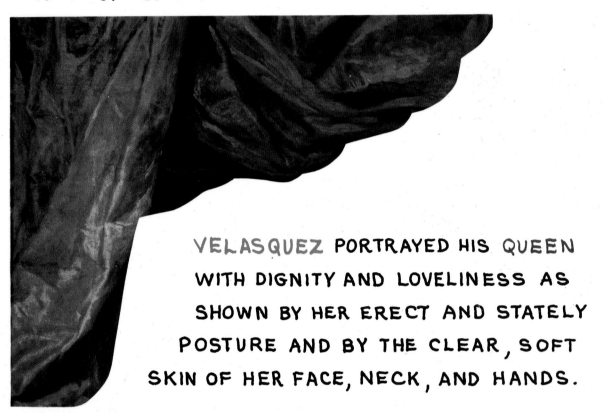

VELASQUEZ PORTRAYED HIS QUEEN
WITH DIGNITY AND LOVELINESS AS
SHOWN BY HER ERECT AND STATELY
POSTURE AND BY THE CLEAR, SOFT
SKIN OF HER FACE, NECK, AND HANDS.

THE STARCHED STIFFNESS OF HER 17TH CENTURY
DRESS IS IN KEEPING WITH THE DIGNITY AND FORMALITY
OF HER EXPRESSION. ONLY THE
GRACEFUL FOLDS OF THE DRAPES
ABOVE AND OF THE WHITE SILK
HANDKERCHIEF GIVE A TOUCH OF
WARMTH
AND
SOFTNESS
TO THE ROYAL PORTRAIT.

DETAIL

MARIANA OF AUSTRIA, QUEEN OF SPAIN   PRADO, MADRID

"PRINCE PHILIP PROSPER", THE YOUNGEST SON OF KING PHILIP IV OF SPAIN, WAS ONE OF THE LAST PAINTINGS DONE BY VELASQUEZ.

DETAIL

WHEN WE STUDY THE FINE DRAPES AND THE RICHLY UPHOLSTERED CHAIR, WE CAN SEE THAT VELASQUEZ TOOK SPECIAL CARE IN PAINTING FABRICS.

THE PRINCE IS SHOWN DRESSED IN STARCHED LINEN AND TINY MUSICAL BELLS. IN THIS VERY FORMAL SETTING, THE SMALL, RELAXED DOG SEEMS TO BE WAITING FOR THE PRINCE TO FINISH WITH HIS TASK OF POSING.

THE BOY'S FACE SEEMS TO SHINE WITH

INNOCENCE.

HAVEN'T YOU SEEN THIS SAME, CLEAR, SEARCHING EXPRESSION ?

PRINCE PHILIP PROSPER   KUNSTHISTORISCHES MUSEUM, VIENNA

IN "THE MAIDS OF HONOR" (CALLED "LAS MENINAS"
IN SPANISH) VELASQUEZ HAS PAINTED A TENDER
STORY OF THE SPANISH COURT.

DETAIL

THE ARTIST SHOWS
HIMSELF WITH HIS
BRUSH AND PALETTE
AT WORK ON A
LIFE-SIZE PORTRAIT
OF KING PHILIP AND
QUEEN MARIANA.
YOU CAN SEE THEM
REFLECTED IN THE
MIRROR HANGING
ON THE BACK WALL
OF THE STUDIO.

THE LITTLE PRINCESS
MARGARITA DOES NOT
WANT TO POSE, EVEN
THOUGH HER ATTENDANT
IS OFFERING HER A
BRIBE. NO ONE IN THE SCENE — HER MAIDS OF HONOR,
THE TWO DWARFS, NOR HER TEACHERS — CAN PERSUADE HER.

VELASQUEZ UNDERSTOOD THIS MOMENT, AND BY
PAINTING THE SCENE JUST AS IT HAPPENED, HE HAS
RECORDED AN INTIMATE GLIMPSE INTO FAMILY LIFE
AT THE ROYAL COURT.

THIS IS ONE OF THE MOST FAMOUS PAINTINGS IN THE
WORLD. VELASQUEZ HAS VIVIDLY CAPTURED THIS
MOMENT OF CHILDHOOD AND MADE IT LIVE ETERNALLY.

THE MAIDS OF HONOR   PRADO, MADRID

THE "INFANTA MARGARITA" WAS NOT QUITE COMPLETED
WHEN VELASQUEZ DIED IN 1660. HIS SON-IN-LAW,
JUAN BATISTA DEL MAZO, FINISHED THE PICTURE.

DETAIL : HEAD

THE RICH COLORS AND THE SWEEPING, CURVING LINES
OF THE BEAUTIFUL GOWN ARE CROWNED BY THE
PRINCESS' THOUGHTFUL, YOUNG FACE.

THE PAINTING'S BRIGHT DETAIL REMINDS US OF THE
BEAUTY IN NATURE AROUND US. OUR IMAGINATION CAN
EASILY TURN THE BLUE SKIRT INTO A FIELD OF SKY
AND THE SPARKLING SILVER BROCADES INTO TRAILS
LEFT BY FALLING STARS.

VELASQUEZ WITH HIS INSIGHT AND MASTERY OF
PAINTING MADE A PRINCESS FROM THE PAST
LIVE FOREVER.

THE INFANTA MARGARITA   KUNSTHISTORISCHES MUSEUM, VIENNA

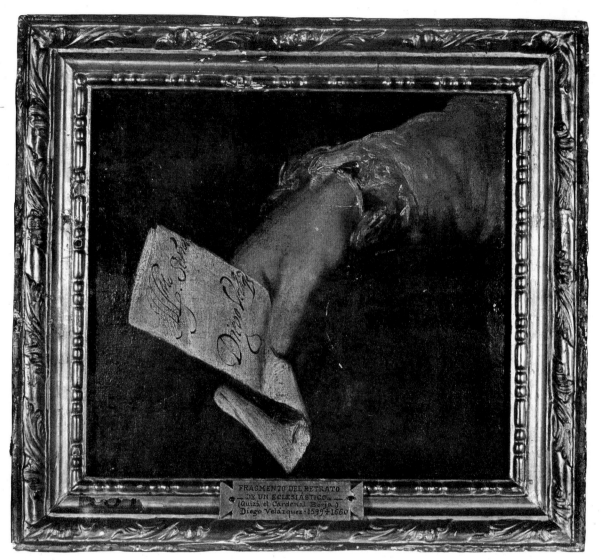

FRAGMENTO DEL RETRATO
DE UN ECLESIÁSTICO
(Quizá el Cardenal Borja.)
Diego Velázquez·1599✝1660

HAND OF A PRIEST   ROYAL PALACE, MADRID